D1032274

JOHN CABOT

Explorer of the North American Mainland

KEISHA HATCHETT

ROSEN PUBLISHING®

New York

Published in 2017 by The Rosen Publishing Group, Inc.
29 East 21st Street, New York, NY 10010

Library of Congress Cataloging-in-Publication Data

Names: Hatchett, Keisha, author.
Title: John Cabot : explorer of the North American mainland / Keisha Hatchett.
Description: New York : Rosen Publishing, 2017. | Series: Spotlight on explorers and colonization | Includes bibliographical references and index. | Audience: Grade 5 to 10.
Identifiers: LCCN 2015050557| ISBN 9781477788165 (library bound) | ISBN 9781477788141 (pbk.) | ISBN 9781477788158 (6-pack)
Subjects: LCSH: Cabot, John, -1498? | America--Discovery and exploration--British. | North America--Discovery and exploration--British. | Explorers--America--Biography. | Explorers--Great Britain--Biography. | Explorers--Italy--Biography.
Classification: LCC E129.C1 H33 2016 | DDC 910.92--dc23
LC record available at http://lccn.loc.gov/2015050557

Manufactured in the United States of America

CONTENTS

WHO WAS JOHN CABOT?

During the Age of Exploration, sailors like Vasco da Gama and Christopher Columbus sought to discover new lands and establish faster trading routes to Asia. Before airplanes and modern ships, people had to rely on big wooden boats with sails that took months to cross the Atlantic Ocean. Among these brave men was a navigator named Giovanni Caboto, best known as John Cabot.

Historians aren't exactly sure about some of the details of his life, but we do know that the Italian explorer set sail to Canada on an expedition for England during the Tudor years. After Columbus landed in what everyone thought was the Indies, he, Cabot, and other explorers looked to reach Asia.

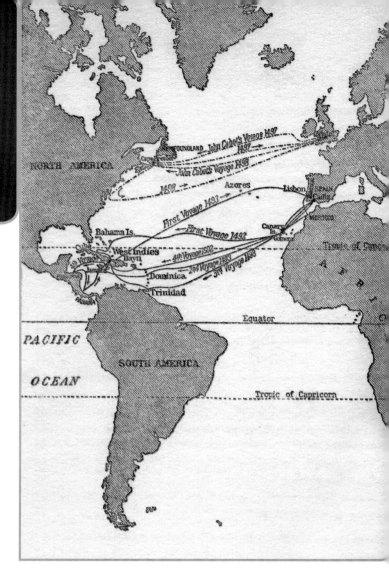

During the booming Age of Exploration, Christopher Columbus and John Cabot made the lengthy trek from Europe to the Americas using several different routes.

Asia was believed to be rich with gold, gems, and other extravagances. With the support of King Henry VII, Cabot traveled across the Atlantic in hopes of finding a shorter route to Asia but landed in a strange place he called "new found land." Today, it's known as Newfoundland, Canada.

THE AGE OF EXPLORATION

The mid-fifteenth and sixteenth centuries saw a number of sailors traveling to uncharted territories, thus earning their title as the Age of Exploration and Discovery. With spices such as pepper, cinnamon, nutmeg, ginger, and cloves, as well as other luxuries from India and the Far East sweeping through Europe, explorers wanted to find a more direct route to obtain such goods.

After Christopher Columbus discovered the Americas (which he thought were the Indies) in 1492, England wanted to take advantage of the opportunity to send its own explorers across the seas. However, England didn't have very many skilled sailors to make

Indian spices were quite popular in the fifteenth and sixteenth centuries. Explorers traveled halfway across the world to obtain them.

the long voyage into the unknown, so King Henry VII looked for others on the continent. John Cabot of Venice volunteered to go on behalf of Britain, and the monarch approved. While the Spanish and Portuguese explorers headed southwest, Cabot decided to travel northwest in hopes of finding a more direct route to Asia.

THE BIRTH OF JOHN CABOT

Christopher Columbus wasn't the only explorer to discover parts of North America. John Cabot is credited with claiming the upper northern territory now known as Canada for the British, but his roots began in Italy. He was born in 1450 in the Italian port of Genoa, the same birthplace as Columbus. He was the son of a spice merchant named Guilo Caboto, and their last name means "coastal seaman" in Italian. You could say he was destined to be an explorer.

He and his family moved to Venice in 1461. Venice was a major trade center at the time. John quickly learned about trading spices from his father. After making connections with Italian sailors who had

already traveled east, he developed the ambition to cut out the middleman and travel the spice trade routes himself.

TRAVELING ABROAD FOR SUPPORT

In Italy, Cabot married a woman named Mattea, and they had three sons together: Ludovico, Sebastiano (Sebastian), and Sancto. Sometime in the 1490s, they all moved to Valencia, Spain. Cabot hoped that he would gain support from the Portuguese or Spanish monarchs to fund a voyage across the Atlantic.

Like Columbus, Cabot believed Asia could be reached by sailing west rather than east. No one would realize that the lands Columbus and others had explored were not Asia until 1502. That year, upon return from a voyage,

King Ferdinand and Queen Isabella of Spain supported Christopher Columbus's trip to the Americas, but they refused to do the same for John Cabot.

explorer Amerigo Vespucci declared that the continent to the west was a New World.

In the 1490s, Cabot was already an experienced seaman, navigator, and spice merchant, so he probably would be a good leader for a westward expedition. Unfortunately, King Ferdinand and Queen Isabella of Spain turned him down because of their commitment to Columbus. That meant Cabot had to try his luck elsewhere.

REJECTION IN PORTUGAL

In Portugal, Cabot again tried to sway monarchs to fund his trip to the Orient, but he arrived too late: Portuguese monarchs had already lent their support to fellow explorers Bartolomeu Dias and Vasco da Gama. Dias became famous for being the first explorer to reach the Indian Ocean from the Atlantic, having sailed around the southernmost tip of Africa to do so. He also discovered the Cape of Good Hope on the journey home. Da Gama followed Dias's route even farther and became the first European to reach India by sea.

With all of these amazing discoveries by other explorers, Cabot hoped to follow in

BARTHOLOMEW DIAZ ON HIS VOYAGE TO THE CAPE

their footsteps. However, there was one thing standing in the way—an approval. King John II of Portugal felt that his country already had enough of its people to send across the sea, so he didn't need to enlist Cabot for the job. Once again, Cabot was out of luck.

FINDING SUPPORT IN ENGLAND

After failing to gain support from Portugal and Spain, Cabot and his family moved to Bristol in England—the perfect place to launch an expedition to the Indies and China via a northwest passage. At this point, no one had yet tried to reach the Far East by sailing northwest from Europe. But Cabot was about to become the first.

Bristol was a major port city with a history of shipbuilding and plenty of experienced sailors close by. Later, the shipbuilding industry would help develop the British navy. In 1588, during the reign of Queen Elizabeth I, England defeated the powerful Spanish

A statue of John Cabot in Bristol, England, is positioned looking out to sea. He moved there with his family in the late 1400s.

armada and established itself as the strongest navy in the world.

For now, Bristol was a place for sailors—especially London-based Italian bankers who agreed to invest in Cabot's trip, as did merchants from Bristol. Smart businessmen, they were looking to expand their trading opportunities after sponsoring previous inquiries into the North Atlantic. It seemed Cabot was the right man for the job.

BACKING FROM KING HENRY VII

With Europe raving about Christopher Columbus's big discovery, King Henry VII needed to take action for Britain. After ascending to the throne in 1485, his reign was threatened by a number of plots and conspiracies. A major discovery would bring not only prosperity to the country but also respect and new land. Spain and Portugal already had a head start, with their explorers claiming land on three continents that would become part of valuable overseas empires. Henry VII wanted England to have the same trade advantages and power. He knew an expedition to the New World would be a good investment.

ATLANTICUS

Carlef Town Fear P.
Carteret P.
Sawanach
GEORGIA
FLORIDA
S. Auguftinuf
Prom. Floridae
CUBA I

ENRICUS VII ANGLIAE REX JOANNEM
BOTAM ET SEBASTIANUM FILIUM
TRONOMIAE REIQ NAUTICAE PERI-
SSIMOS ANNO MCCCCXCVI NAVA-
HOS INSTITUIT SUIS LITTERISQUI
AM INVENIRENT QUAM ANIMO
ITABANT AD INDOS ORIENTA-

In this painting of Henry VII, Cabot and two of his sons are shown to the right. Cabot's son Sebastiano (Sebastian) would later follow in his father's exploring footsteps.

The king granted Cabot permission to set sail and discover new islands and countries in the west, east, and north on March 5, 1496. Even though the king had not personally financed the trip, he stood to gain one-fifth of all merchandise brought back.

FIRST TREK ACROSS THE ATLANTIC

With the backing of England and with excitement for Asia fresh in the air, Cabot's first attempt was considered a failure. Historians aren't sure about what exactly happened on that unofficial journey in 1496. There are no surviving records from the ship's logs or written first-hand accounts from the sailors on board.

The information we do have comes from a letter that John Day, an English merchant in the Spanish trade, wrote to Christopher Columbus in 1497. In it, he said that "he [Cabot] went with one ship, he had a disagreement with the crew, he was short of

Fellow Italian explorer Christopher Columbus set sail for America with three ships: the *Niña*, the *Pinta*, and the *Santa María*. He made landfall in 1492.

food and ran into bad weather, and he decided to turn back." Though Cabot's first journey across the Atlantic ended before he discovered new lands, he was determined to try again.

CABOT'S SECOND ATTEMPT

On May 2, 1497, Cabot made his second attempt to sail from Bristol on a single ship named *Matthew*. Likely named after his wife, Mattea, the vessel carried a small crew of eighteen across the Atlantic Ocean. His three sons also joined him for the two-month journey, which was not easy.

Sailors faced poor hygiene, bug-infested food, and contaminated drinking water. This lack of healthy food and water often caused sailors to contract diseases such as typhoid fever and scurvy. Typhoid fever is caused by the bacteria *Salmonella typhi*. In addition to high fevers, it can cause a rash of pink spots. Scurvy results from a lack of vitamin C, which was common in sailors because they didn't have access to fresh fruits and vegetables.

With other threats such as incredibly rough storms, it wasn't uncommon for a portion of the crew to die on long sea journeys. But experienced seamen like Cabot were fully aware of the risks involved. He was determined to find the Northwest Passage to Asia.

MAKING LANDFALL IN CANADA

Cabot's journey to the west was a lot shorter than Christopher Columbus's. Columbus, who sailed closer to the equator, relied on faulty mathematics that led him to believe Earth's circumference was a lot smaller than it actually was. His journey from Spain to the Caribbean was around 4,000 miles (6,400 kilometers).

Instead, Cabot traveled around Ireland and then north and west. He made landfall on the morning of June 24 after traveling about 2,300 miles (3,700 km) during less than two months at sea. Scholars can't

Cabot and his crew arrived in Newfoundland, Canada, in 1497. Historians never determined where exactly he and his crew made landfall.

agree on where exactly he landed. The belief is that he either made it to what is now southern Labrador, Newfoundland, or Cape Breton Island. What everyone can agree on, however, is that Cabot landed on what is now called Canada.

EXPLORING A NEW LAND

When the astronauts from Apollo 11 placed the American flag on the moon in 1969, they were taking a page from early explorers like Cabot, who used flags to claim land for the nations that had sponsored their expeditions. After landing in present-day Newfoundland, Cabot placed the British flag in the soil, claiming the land for Britain.

He still believed the new land to be part of Asia, which it certainly was not. Exploring this unknown world, he traveled along the coastline and began naming places like Cape Discovery, Island of St. John, St. George's Cape, the Trinity Islands, and England's Cape. Today, they're known as

The Cabot Trail, named after the Italian explorer, stretches around the northern tip of Cape Breton Island in Newfoundland.

Cape North, St. Paul Island, Cape Ray, St. Pierre and Miquelon, and Cape Race. The water between Newfoundland and Cape Breton Island, which connects the Atlantic Ocean to the Gulf of St. Lawrence along the Canadian mainland, is now named Cabot Strait, after Cabot.

MAKING A CLAIM FOR ENGLAND

With very few records in Cabot's log, the surviving documentation of his discovery comes from letters by Raimondo Soncino, Duke of Milano, and Lorenzo Pasqualigo, a merchant of Venice, who were both living in London at the time. Bristol merchant John Day also described Cabot's exploits to Christopher Columbus in a letter from the winter of 1497–98.

According to Day, Cabot spotted the strange land and soon raised a cross along with the banner of England. He wrote, "Your Lordship will know that he landed at only one spot of the mainland, near the place

DISCOVERY OF NORTH AMERICA BY JOHN AND SEBASTIAN CABOT

where land was first sighted, and they disembarked there with a crucifix and raised banners with the arms of the Holy Father and those of the King of England." Cabot and his men became the first Europeans to set foot on North America since the Vikings' short-lived settlement on Newfoundland five hundred years earlier.

DISCOVERING REMNANTS OF THE BEOTHUK

Embarking on an inland trail filled with grass and tall trees, Cabot and his men found that the area had previously been inhabited. They discovered a site where a fire had been made and saw animal droppings that might have belonged to a farmer's herd.

The crew stumbled upon a 1.5-foot-long (0.46-meter-long) stick that was pierced at both ends and painted, possibly belonging to a tribe called the Beothuk. Unlike on other explorers' journeys, there are no recorded encounters between Cabot's men and the natives of the land. Not much is known about the Beothuk, a hunter-gatherer tribe.

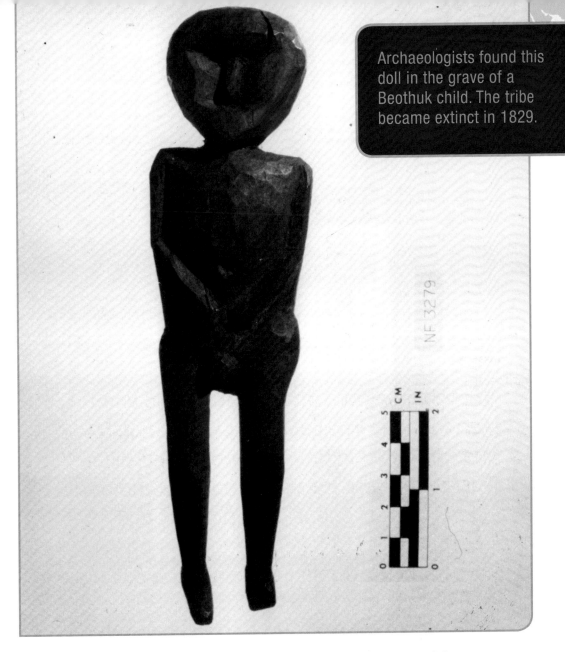

Archaeologists found this doll in the grave of a Beothuk child. The tribe became extinct in 1829.

NF 3279

Not wanting to take any chances with native people, Cabot collected fresh drinking water before leading his men back to the ship and opting for travel along the coast by sea.

A SEA FULL OF CODFISH

Traveling down the coast, Cabot and his man found an endless supply of codfish (the English called them stockfish). This was great news for the explorers, who had a limited meat supply and buggy bread. Cabot is said to have reported that there were so many fish in the sea that he could dip his basket in the ocean to catch them. Today, there aren't as many fish in the sea. In 2013, researchers found that after decades of overfishing, the supply of codfish was running extremely low and might not ever recover.

After a month of exploring by boat, Cabot and his men found no gold or riches, which they might have seen had they landed in the markets of Asia as they intended. They headed back to England on July 20, 1497.

In Cabot's time, codfish were abundant in the North Atlantic and could be plucked from the water in baskets. Today, there aren't as many left because of overfishing.

RETURNING HOME A HERO

The Italian explorer arrived back in Bristol on August 6, 1497, and received a hero's welcome. Despite not finding the gold, spices, and other luxuries he hoped for, Cabot returned home with something much better. He reported a temperate climate, excellent land, and enough fish to end England's reliance on importing from Iceland. This was perfect timing because Iceland had experienced a plague epidemic two years prior.

For the successful journey discovering new land and a new food source, King Henry VII rewarded Cabot with a cash bonus and annual pension. Soon after, Cabot announced plans to follow up with a larger expedition. The king, eager for more land in and products from the New World, granted his wish.

Cabot returned to England a hero as the leader of England's first successful voyage to the New World. He was gifted with money and high praise from the king.

THE FINAL JOURNEY

Cabot embarked on his third and final voyage across the sea on February 3, 1498. This time his aim was to discover Japan. While his first two tries were with one ship, he was now in command of five ships and about three hundred men. That's a big difference from the crew of eighteen with which he traveled on his first journey.

The fleet made its way north to Greenland, which Cabot named Labrador's Land. After running into extremely cold weather and icebergs, one damaged ship had to sail to Ireland for refuge. Four hundred years later, another famous vessel would face

Despite its name, there's not much green in Greenland. About 80 percent of the country is covered in ice.

irreparable damage from icebergs in the North Atlantic—the *Titanic*. One ship down, the remaining fleet pushed farther south.

CROSSING THE DAVIS STRAIT

John Cabot crossed the Davis Strait before proceeding on to Baffin Island and then Newfoundland. The journey was especially difficult because of how cold the weather was and the fact that supplies were running low. Located between Greenland and Baffin Island, the strait sees heavy ice movement, which meant Cabot's men would have been on the lookout for icebergs. If his remaining ships were to sink after encountering one, they would have reached depths as low as 12,000 feet (3,660 meters)!

Following the coast to what is now Nova Scotia and New England, he sought out the rich lands filled with spices and other luxuries he envisioned back home. However, he only found troubling weather and was soon forced to head back home to England.

Davis Strait lies between Greenland and Baffin Island and sees heavy ice movement, which presents a danger for ships trying to cross it.

AN EXPLORER LOST AT SEA

Scholars can't agree on what happened to John Cabot after he decided to sail back to England. By 1499, he was believed to be dead. Some say his son Sancto and a few members of his crew perished while ashore and that Cabot may have died at sea.

The news that Cabot's ships had not returned to England reached the Spanish government by June 8, 1501, and the Spanish quickly jumped into action. With Cabot out of the way, they had the opportunity to explore in the northern areas where Cabot had been. Letters were issued to Alonso de Ojeda to explore the coasts of the Caribbean, from south to north, ending in Colombia. He was told to follow the coast that would lead him to the area where Cabot had made his discoveries, because the Spanish wanted to stop the English from exploring further in that area.

Sebastian Cabot explains his findings to King Henry VII. Following in his father's footsteps, he underwent several expeditions in the early sixteenth century.

CABOT'S LEGACY

Although he didn't find the riches he was looking for, Cabot's discoveries had a huge impact on British colonization in North America. More explorers made the trek across the Atlantic Ocean, including Humphrey Gilbert, the man behind England's first attempt to settle on the new continent; Martin Frobisher, who discovered Frobisher Bay; Henry Hudson, who discovered Hudson Bay; and William Baffin, who discovered Baffin Island.

After more than a century of exploration in North America, England shifted focus toward

moving settlers into its new land claims. In 1607, England established its first permanent overseas colony, Jamestown, in what is now Virginia. Cabot's son Sebastian continued his legacy by sailing the Hudson Strait and exploring the East Coast. It's because of these early British claims, led by Cabot, that most people speak English in North America today.

GLOSSARY

Beothuk An extinct tribe native to Newfoundland.

conspiracies Secret plans made by two or more people to commit wrongful acts.

contaminated To make something impure by mixing it with something unclean.

crucifix A cross with the image of Jesus Christ on it, considered to be a religious item.

disembarked Headed to shore from a ship.

hygiene The practice of staying healthy and clean.

inhabited Occupied by people or animals.

luxuries Items that are considered extravagant.

merchant Someone who buys or sells goods for a profit; a trader.

monarchs People who hold power over a nation, such as kings, queens, or emperors.

navigator A person who goes on explorations by sea.

overfishing To fish so much that the supply becomes critically low.

pension A fixed amount of money paid regularly to a person for a period of time.

scholars Educated people with expert knowledge on a subject.

seaman A person skilled in handling, sailing, and navigating a ship during a voyage.

uncharted An unknown place not shown on a map.

John Cabot University
Via della Lungara 233
00165 Rome
Italy
Website: http://www.johncabot.edu
John Cabot University is a liberal arts university based
    in Cabot's home country of Italy. Its extensive
    library database offers information on the explorer.

Mariners' Museum
100 Museum Drive
Newport News, VA 23606
(757) 596-2222
Website: http://www.marinersmuseum.org
The Mariners' Museum provides ship models, rare
    books, illustrations, maps, navigational instruments,
    and other artifacts from the Age of Discovery.

Maritime Museum of British Columbia
634 Humboldt Street
Victoria, BC V8W 1A6
Canada
(250) 382-2869
Website: http://www.mmbc.bc.ca
The Maritime Museum of British Columbia has
    a collection of logbooks, personal papers,
    photographs, and other items from explorations.

Metropolitan Museum of Art
1000 Fifth Avenue (at 82nd Street)
New York, NY 10028
(212) 535-7710
Website: http://www.metmuseum.org
The Metropolitan Museum of Art has a collection of
    clothing, clocks, and other scientific instruments
    from the Age of Discovery.

Newfoundland Historical Society
5 Hallett Crescent
St. John's, NL A1B 4C4
Canada
(709) 722-3191
Website: http://www.nlhistory.ca
The Newfoundland Historical Society provides a
    series of lectures and discussions on the history
    and heritage of Newfoundland and Labrador.

Websites

Because of the changing nature of Internet links, Rosen
Publishing has developed an online list of websites
related to the subject of this book. This site is updated
regularly. Please use this link to access the list:

http://www.rosenlinks.com/SEC/cabot

FOR FURTHER READING

Dalrymple, Lisa. *Explore with John Cabot* (Travel with the Great Explorers). New York, NY: Crabtree Publishing Company, 2015.

Doak, Robin. *Cabot: John Cabot and the Journey to North America* (Exploring the World). Mankato, MN: Capstone Press, 2003.

Garfield, Henry. *The Lost Voyage of John Cabot.* New York, NY: Simon Pulse, 2007.

Hunter, Douglas. *The Race to the New World: Christopher Columbus, John Cabot, and a Lost History of Discovery.* New York, NY: St. Martin's Griffin, 2012.

Krull, Kathleen. *Lives of the Explorers: Discoveries, Disasters (and What the Neighbors Thought).* Boston, MA: HMH Books for Young Readers, 2014.

Matthews, Rupert. *DK Eyewitness Books: Explorer.* New York, NY: DK Children, 2012.

Ross, Stewart. *Into the Unknown: How Great Explorers Found Their Way by Land, Sea, and Air.* Somerville, MA: Candlewick Press, 2014.

BIBLIOGRAPHY

The Caboto Trail. "The History of Giovanni Caboto, A.k.a. John Cabot." Retrieved December 16, 2015 (http://www.thecabototrail.com/index.html).

Dictionary of Canadian Biography. "Cabot, John." Retrieved December 16, 2015 (http://www.biographi.ca/en/bio/cabot_john_1E.html).

The Gilder Lehrman Institute of American History. "The Age Of Exploration." *History Now*, Vol. 12, Summer 2007 (http://www.gilderlehrman.org/history-now/2007-06/age-exploration).

The Mariners' Museum. "The Ages of Exploration." Retrieved December 16, 2015 (http://exploration.marinersmuseum.org/).

Mysteries of Canada. "What Happened to the Beothuk Indians?" October 30, 2014. Retrieved December 16, 2015 (http://www.mysteriesofcanada.com/newfoundland/beothuk/).

Newfoundland and Labrador Heritage. "John Cabot." Retrieved December 16, 2015 (http://www.heritage.nf.ca/articles/exploration/john-cabot.php).

Thomson, Aly. "Some Species Won't Bounce Back." *Huffington Post*, April 18, 2013 (http://www.huffingtonpost.ca/2013/04/18/canada-overfishing-cod-stock_n_3111173.html).

Watkins, Thayer. "The Spanish and Portuguese Conquest of the Americas." San Jose State University. Retrieved December 16, 2015 (http://www.sjsu.edu/faculty/watkins/theconquest.htm).

INDEX

About the Author

Keisha Hatchett always knew she would be a writer, which is why she earned a degree in English literature from Florida Atlantic University. She has always been a fan of history and spent most of her childhood learning about the real events surrounding the *Titanic's* 1912 disaster. She also has a background in journalism and has been published in *Entertainment Weekly* several times. She is originally from Florida but now lives and writes in New York City. This is her first book published, but certainly not the last.

Photo Credits

Designer: Nicole Russo; Editor: Meredith Day; Photo Researcher: Karen Huang